ALDOUS THANE

THE GIFT OF FEARS

**The Ultimate Guide on How to Face Your Fears,
Discover the Most Common Fears And Tips on
How to Overcome Them**

Descrierea CIP a Bibliotecii Naţionale a României
ALDOUS THANE
    THE GIFT OF FEARS. The Ultimate Guide on How to Face Your Fears, Discover the Most Common Fears And Tips on How to Overcome Them / Aldous Thane – Bucharest: Editura My Ebook, 2021
    ISBN

ALDOUS THANE

THE GIFT OF FEARS

The Ultimate Guide on How to Face Your Fears, Discover the Most Common Fears And Tips on How to Overcome Them

My Ebook Publishing House
Bucharest, 2021

CONTENTS

INTRODUCTION

This book will cover the topic of facing fear so the first thing you need to know is what is classified a fear? The definition of the word 'fear' is:

an unpleasant emotion caused by the threat of danger, pain, or harm.

It also means:

To be afraid of something or someone

Fears come in all sizes and with varying depths of intensity. No two people are going to demonstrate the same type of fear to the same thing. This is one reason why facing your fears can be difficult. As quite often the first step is to acknowledge and admit that you have the fear in the first place.

Fear is a survival instinct and without it humans would have not survive life--threatening situations. Fear keeps us alive by alerting us to imminent dangers. When humans feared the right things, they survive and pass these traits on to the next generation.

Some fears are cooked into our genes. Have you ever been bitten by a snake, probably not, and yet you are fearful of snakes. Why don't you walk down a dark alley at night? Your internal warning system anticipates danger. There may be something hiding in the shadows.

Throughout this book we will talk about various areas of fears and each section will finish with Exercises or Actionable Steps that you can use to help you face your fears.

How Fears Work and Examples of Common Fears

Fear is explained as a chain reaction that begins in your brain. A stressful situation begins these events your brain is stimulated and releases chemicals that cause your heart to start racing. You no doubt have experienced these feelings at some point. Your mind is racing and your heart feels as though it's going to pop right out of your chest!

Your heart is racing heart, your breathing quickens and your muscles start to react. Your body wants to flee from the situation. This response of your body is actually termed the Flight or Fight Response.

There are so many different things that can stimulate your body into this response. Some common fears are spiders, a fear of heights, having to fly, being in a crowded room or facing someone with a knife or gun in their hands. Even a sudden loud noise or unaccepted turn of events in a movie can trigger your body into action.

It is important to understand that your brain is a complex organ. It contains more than 100 billion nerve cells, these cells serve as your communication system for everything that you sense, think and do. You don't always control all of these events and while you do make conscious actions your body also responds automatically. This is termed an Autonomic Response and when this happens you often don't have control until the event has happened.

Researchers have identified that there are two paths your mind can take when it comes to fear.

1. Low Road
2. High Road

The low road is described as the quick and messy route. This would be when your autonomic response kicks into gear and takes over. Basically you are reacting before you are thinking.

The high road is where you take the time to define the situation. Did the window open because a storm is approaching or do you have someone lurking outside your home? Basically you are considering your options before you take action.

Common Fears

The most common fears amongst people today include:

- Acts of Terrorism

- Spiders
- Death
- Failure
- Heights
- Crime
- Being alone
- The Future
- War
- Cancer
- Snakes

Many people can relate to these fears but fears can be different depending upon where you live. People who live in the mountains of Switzerland may be more fearful of avalanches. People in Florida fear hurricanes while people in other parts of the world fear earthquakes or tornadoes.

Statistics for Common Fears

Because so many fears affect numerous people medical terms have been applied to some of the most popular:

1. Fear of Public Speaking: ttlossophobia – affects 74% of business people in the U.S. today.

2. Fear of Death: Necrophobia – affects 68% of the U.S. Population

3. Fear of Spiders: Arachnophobia – affects 30.5% of the U.S. Population

4. Fear of Darkness: Achluophoiba, Acotophobia or Myctophobia–affects 11% of the U.S. Population

5. Fear of Heights: Acrophobia – affects 10% of the U.S. Population

6. Fear of Social Situations/people: Sociophobia – affects 7.9% of the U.S. Population

7. Fear of Flying Aerophobia: affects 6.5% of the U.S. Population

8. Fear of Confined Spaces, Claustrophobia: 2.5% of the U.S. Population

9. Fear of Open Spaces, Agoraphobia: affects 2.2% of the U.S. Population

10. Fear of Thunder and Lightning: Brontophobia affects 2% of the U.S. Population

While living with fear is very common place, serious problems begin to develop when these fears turn into chronic fears. A chronic fear is something that you just can't get out of your head, no matter what. You find yourself constantly thinking about this thing all the time and fear it intensely.

If you develop this type of fear you should visit your doctor and seek treatment and possibly counseling to overcome your fears. This type of fear is not healthy at all and could lead to developing severe anxiety and/or depression.

How to Expose Your Fears

It is very common for you to not want to face your fears. Most people prefer not to even speak about their fears. There is a process to facing your fears and this is known as **Exposing** your fears.

Exposing your fears involves gradually going into those situations that make you fearful. This is a slow process where you place yourself in a certain instance for a very small amount of time. Over time you will start to feel less anxious about facing this particular situation and this helps to reduce your fear of it.

This process works the best when you begin by facing a situation that makes you fearful, but not one that you are terrified of. By facing your smaller fears first, you can build up to facing and exposing larger ones.

For example, you are afraid of going into pools of water, but want to learn how to swim. You don't jump head first into a pool. Instead, on your first few visits, you learn how to get closer to the pool. Your next step is to place your feet in the pool, then you try putting more of your body into the pool until you are able to go into the pool all the way. From here you take small steps to learn how to swim, including putting your face under water.

It really helps to make a list of your fears as well as to identify your ultimate goal by conquering a fear. You can then plan out all the baby steps needed to take to face and overcome the fear. You do not need to do this on a daily basis, exposing yourself to your fear once a week or even once a month may be sufficient in the beginning.

As your fears lessen you may discover that you are ready to take more action more often. It never hurts to reward yourself after you have taken action. Select something such as a book, a DVD or going out to dinner with a friend as your reward for taking action.

Exposing Your Fears Exercises

Step 1: In order to face your fears you need to identify them first. In the chart below, list out your top 5 fears that you want to conquer. List them from the least fearful to the one you fear the most.

14

Name of Fear
1.
2.
3.
4.
5.

Your next step involves taking baby steps to conquer this fear.

Take the first fear that you listed above and write out 4 or 5 steps that you can putinto action to help you face this fear. Set a time limit for each exercise. It is often helpful to choose a particular place to face your fear. As in our example above this would be at a swimming pool. Also decide if this is something that you can do alone or if you would prefer to have a friend with you.

Fear 1.	Date	Goal	Baby Steps	Time Limit	Environment	Help Needed

Fear 1.	Date	Goal	Baby Steps	Time Limit	Environment	Help Needed
Step 1.						
Step 2						
Step 3.						
Step 4						

As you face your fear, fill in the columns and make note of how long you were exposed to your fear. You may want to start small with just 30 seconds and then work up to more. Record your progress on the worksheet. Documenting your progress is an important step of overcoming fears and anxieties.

16

Panic Attacks

A panic attack is also referred to as an acute fear. All of a sudden, without any type of warning, you are riddled with fear. You feel as though the world is spinning and you don't feel as though you are there. It is an unreal feeling where your heart is beating like crazy and you often feel as though you may die.

These attacks can leave you confused, embarrassed and afraid. You don't really know why they occurred and all you want to do is run home and hide. You become fearful of going out again in order to avoid the terror should it reoccur.

Many people suffer from panic attacks very infrequently, but some experience them on a much higher level more often. Actually 2.7% of all Americans aged over 18 suffer from this disorder. It is actually more common than schizophrenia and bipolar disorders.

A panic attack varies in its severity and length. An attack could last for just one or two minutes or they could last up to 30 minutes. When these attacks occur too often then it is possible that it turns into Agoraphobia – the fear of going out in public.

Symptoms of a Panic Attack

In order to be diagnosed with suffering from panic attacks you need to show at least four of the following symptoms. This guide was set by the Diagnostic and Statistical Manual of Mental Disorders.

- Pounding of the heart
- Uncontrollable shaking
- Feeling dizzy
- Sweating profusely
- Feeling as though you are going to choke
- Nausea
- Shallow breathing
- Experiencing chest pain
- Experiencing numbness or tingling
- Suffer from chills
- Suffer from hot flashes

- Feel as though you are going crazy
- Don't feel as though you are really there
- Feel as though you might die

It usually takes experiencing four panic attacks within a four week period to bediagnosed with a panic attack.

Of course the question remains as to why your body suddenly reacts this way. A panic attack works in almost the same manner as a fear. When you become frightened or fearful, your nervous system takes over. A panic attack causes your muscles to get tense while your hormones release adrenaline into your bloodstream. This makes your chest and your throat feel tight and you may even feel as though you can't breathe properly.

What you are experiencing during a panic attack is simply a reaction from your body. The worst part is that you don't understand what caused this sudden attackand this is what makes you feel as though you may be going crazy.

Panic attacks and anxiety attacks are both terms used to describe the same situation although a panic attack is thought of as lasting for a shorter time period.

What Causes Your Panic Attack?

When suffering from a panic attack your brain is doing the same thing as it would when you are dealing with a known fear. To date there is no known exact cause of a panic attack, but there are some theories on this subject.

Quite often a life changing event can cause some people to suffer from panic attacks. Most of these attacks can be linked to stressful situations in people's lives. They can also be linked back to events that have happened in childhood.

Panic attacks often occur in people who are overly tired. This is because your brain produces carbon dioxide when you are tired. When these levels increase they send a signal to your brain causing your airways to constrict making it difficult to breathe. You start to feel as though you are suffocating which causes your breathing rate to speed up. This rapid increase triggers a panic attack.

Young adults in their twenties are the age group who suffer panic attacks more so than other age groups. Usually more women than men suffer from them, and it is not uncommon for children to have panic attacks.

While there are several treatment methods for severe panic attacks, some of them can lead to drug dependency. Antidepressants have been used, but they also lead to undesirable side effects.

One of the preferred treatment methods is cognitive behavioral therapy as this consists of five treatment sections. The patient is educated on panic attacks and their causes and treatments. This is known as the Learning Step.

The second step is the Monitoring one where patients start to keep a record of their symptoms. Knowing when and where they occur is really helpful.

The third step is the Breathing Step. Patients are taught breathing exercises which they can do when an attack starts.

The fourth step is the Rethinking Step where the patient changes their perception of the panic attack.

The fifth and final step is the Exposure Step. This is where the patient slowly learns how to face and deal with the situations that cause the attacks.

As mentioned earlier, most people who suffer from panic attacks are stressed out. This means that your body is tense and you may be bottling up your feelings inside yourself.

Use these simple tips to help yourself reduce your chances of experiencing a panic attack.

- Exercise more often

- Learn how to relax and make time to relax. Yoga classes can be extremely effective for this

- Drink less coffee, sugar and stop smoking

- Learn how to express your feelings

- Don't allow self doubt to creep into your thoughts

Dealing with a Panic Attack

Experiencing a panic attack can truly be a terrifying experience. While you may not always be able to prevent an attack there are some things that you can do to make them easier to deal with.

1. Accept that what you are experiencing is a panic attack and acknowledge that it will pass

2. Repeatedly tell yourself that you are okay and that you are not going to die

3. Slow down your breathing

If you happen to be around a person who is suffering from a panic attack you can help them out by talking to them. Tell them that this will pass and that you are right there for them. Encourage them to slow their breathing down by constantly talking to them and perform deep breathing exercises with them.

22

Panic Attack - Exercises

1. Practice this deep breathing exercise so that when you do experience a panic attack you know how to avert an impending attack.

1. Lie on your back and place pillows under your knees and head
2. Place one hand on your stomach and the other on your chest
3. Slowly breathe in with your stomach rising, but with your chest still
4. Slowly breathe out as you tighten your stomach muscles

2. Write out 3 steps that you can take the next time you feel a panic attack coming on. Practice performing these steps regularly so that when necessary they will be easier to do.

1.

_____

2.

_____

3.

_____

Why Do We Fear Ourselves?

One fear that many people have is a fear of who they are and of what they know. Self improvement is an endless quest for many people who are striving to be the person they think, or have been told, they should become.

The sad fact is that everyone has a multitude of gifts that they don't recognize as such. The issue is for you to recognize them and feel confident about them. When you stop and take a good look inside yourself, you may find that there isn't that much that needs fixing.

Try to uncover what your gifts are that you already possess. You may feel happy about where you live, you have a loving family or you may be a wonderful listener. Other gifts include being true to yourself and others. When asked for an opinion you simply reply with your honest thoughts.

Not all of these things are taken in the right manner by everyone. All of a sudden you are being told that you shouldn't do or say this. You are told that you should think before you speak and worse.

When you hear these things repeatedly you start to believe in them. You begin to look for ways to improve yourself!

Instead of succumbing to pressure to change, take the time to discover your inner gifts. Then learn ways to display these traits with confidence. Yes, this can be easier said than done, but by doing so you are conquering a fear and improving your self confidence and your self esteem.

Let's take a quick look at some gifts that you may fear.

Surprisingly, some people are fearful of their gift to love. Love and passion run deeply in all of our lives, sometimes he intensity of these feelings can be overwhelming or downright intimidating.

How many times have you found yourself reacting fiercely when someone you love is put in danger or threatened? This power can be scary because you may feel as though you are the one frightening others.

Many parents often tell their children to not wear their emotions on their sleeves, or are told to tone things down. Children and teens often feel as though their passion gets them into trouble. So they start to suppress these feelings instead and that is not always a healthy choice either. It is one way for a child's self esteem to become drained.

Vulnerability is another gift or trait that goes directly to your core. Who doesn't have sympathy and feelings for others when things go wrong? Who doesn't cry at the sad parts in a movie? Everyone is sensitive what differs is how much of this sensitivity you allow to show.

Children are instructed to toughen up and not be such a "cry baby." So they stifle their emotions and even fear showing their feelings. Some people naturally feel emotions more deeply than others and this can lead to children and teens becoming the target of bullies. They are viewed as sissy's and are made to feel alone and different to everyone else.

Another question many people want answered is who they are and what makes them different to everyone else? This boils down to your originality. Like snowflakes, everyone is different, unique. Honestly the world would be a boring place if everyone was identical.

For many people these concerns over who they are can be deeply seeded. They often wonder if they will fit in or if they will ever find someone to love them.

Instead of allowing their originality to shine through, they often go the opposite route to hide themselves behind a mask.

If you feel that any of the above applies to you, you need to remember that these qualities are your gifts. It is what makes you unique so you don't want to allow anyone to rob you of these things.

In order to appreciate your own originality you need to uncover your fear and start to love yourself. You can do this by incorporating the following exercises into your life on a regular basis.

Why We Fear Ourselves - Exercises

Use the following section to write down your answers to the questions. In order for this work you must be totally honest with yourself.

Questions:

1. Which gift do you fear the most... love & passion, sensitivity & tenderness or originality?

_____

_____

_____

_____

_____

_____

2. Why do you fear this? Were you bullied or told not to show your emotions as a child?

_____

_____

_____

_____

_____

_____

_____

3. How are you prepared to face and deal with this? A good example of this is if you are afraid to show your feelings, are you ready to tell someone that you love them and if so how will you do this? Remember showing your feelings doesn't always have to be done verbally. You could send someone a note or send them a gift.

_____

_____

_____

_____

_____

_____

_____

4. Set a time and date to do this. As you perform this exercise remember to enjoy it. View it as your act of liberation!

_____

_____

_____

_____

_____

_____

_____

_____

Your Self Doubt

Often, people struggle with self doubt and this is often viewed as fear. How many times have you struggled with certain areas of your life, you suddenly feel the need to defend your action? When this happens the seeds of self doubt are slowing taking root inside your mind.

Self doubt appears at inopportune moments. It may appear when you are out with friends or when you are taking a shower. Your mood changes and you may even start to cry for no apparent reason. How do you get over this fear of self doubt?

Once self doubt starts working its way into your thoughts then your self confidence becomes shaky. The trick is to not allow this to happen, you need to overcome this fear and you are the only person that can do so.

Here's an example of self doubt. After joining a mastermind group or a course to upgrade your skills you immediately start regretting the decision. Questions like: Can I really do this? Am I good enough? Will the others in the group think I am weak? Am I wasting my money?

The correct path of action is to embrace your decision and treat it as a goal that you set yourself. In essence you are taking a leap of faith. You are trusting in your own abilities that you are good enough to see this through.

Self Doubt - Exercises

Use the following questions to expose and conquer your self-doubt. Your answers may just surprise you.

1. Write out a list of your own doubts about your competencies or skills. Place them in order with the strongest one listed first. These can be associated with your personal life, goals, hobbies or work related.

A

_____

B

_____

C

_____

D

_____

E

_____

F

_____

2. Identify a one of your core strengths. This is often difficult for people to do. Think about things that you have helped people with, have you helped someone pass an exam or achieve a goal?

_____

_____

_____

_____

3. Next trying saying your strengths out loud and then read your list of self-doubts. Try to notice which ones you spoke with more force?

_____

_____

_____

_____

Most people **notice** that their self-doubts are vocalized more strongly. This is part of human nature as it is always easier for people to put themselves down, than speak in favor of themselves.

Repeat this exercise several times until you start believing firmly and appreciating the strengths that you have.

Fears and Phobias

Fears and phobias have the potential to ruin your life if you allow them too.

Common fears include the fear of flying, a fear of water or spiders, snakes and even birds!

All fears produce symptoms which can range in intensity. A fear may cause you to have a light or queasy stomach, your breathing may increase, your mouth may go dry, you may be frozen in place or you could start to sweat excessively.

What you want to understand is that you do have a certain amount of control over the way you feel. While this may be difficult to accept you can learn to change the way you feel about your fear.

Fears and phobias can be classified into two main categories:

1. Rational fears
2. Irrational fears

Some fears are known to be survival fears or instincts and this is a normal reaction of being placed in danger or in harm's way. Phobias usually produce irrational fears. These are the types of fear that you know make no sense but your body reacts to them anyway in an extremely intense fashion.

It is possible to turn off your fear by changing the way you think. When you think about it, your mind turns your fear on in the first place, so why can you not turn it off?

Let's say you are frightened of heights. Instead of telling yourself that you will fall off the edge of a mountain, change your thoughts. Tell yourself that the view from the top is a wonderful thing. The ground is solid underfoot and you can stand back a few feet from the edge. The only way you can fall is to jump and that's not in the game plan.

What you are doing is challenging your fears. One tactic is to review statistics on certain events. Ask the park ranger how many people have fell off the top of the mountain accidentally. This quiets your fears. Once you review statistics you find that your mind is making up stories, not reality.

Fears and phobias are normally associated with bad consequences. But there are times when people have been spurred into action because of fear. They have run into a burning building to save someone, or helped pull someone from car wreckage. When faced with fear you do not always flee from the situation.

Sometimes you find the courage to face the fear and take action.

There are many feelings which are associated with fear and sometimes it is necessary to evoke bad feelings in others to overcome something that you fear. You may be in a relationship that has no future and you fear breaking up because you know you are going to cause heartbreak in the other person. This can be very difficult to deal with but eventually your life will become better and your fear will have been faced.

You want to remember this when it comes to dealing with all of your fears. Fear can cripple you if you allow it. Is it worth staying in a bad relationship or dealing with an unhealthy job because of fear?

Fear can evoke feelings of sadness, stress and tears, but once dealt with it can evoke feelings of happiness, laughter and joy!

Some fears and phobia are instilled during childhood. You may have been left to care for a brother or sister while one parent was at work, the other parent may have been abusive or violent. This left you fearful of being left alone with the abusive parent.

Children who never met their parent's expectations may feel like failures or unworthy. As an adult, they feel as though they don't deserve great things and are afraid to set goals to achieve greatness.

Complete the following exercises to help you uncover your fears.

Fear and Phobia Exercises:

1. Make a list of your fears and phobias and list them as rational or irrational.

Rational Based Fears	Irrational Based Fears

2. Next decide on an action to take and add any feelings that may be evoked by doing so. Are you frightened of being alone or not graduating? List the tools you know you have that can help you deal with this. For being alone it can be taking photos or letters with you.

37

Fear	Reaction Evoked	Tools on Hand

3. Look up statistics and facts on your fear and write them out.

Fear

_____

Statistics

_____

4. Now write out the action which is right for you. This could be finding ways to end a relationship or planning on a career change or moving to a new part of thecountry.

_____

_____

_____

Is Your Fear All in Your Mind?

This is a question that is often asked by people including those with and without the fear. How do you know if the fear is all in your mind or not?

As a child you probably experienced all kinds of fears because of your imagination. Were you afraid to get up in the dark to go to the bathroom because the boogey man might get you? These types of fears may have been brought on by a movie you watched or because an older sibling always told you this would happen. The good part is that most of these fears are often outgrown by adulthood if not sooner.

Some fears include imagining yourself buying that new home and living happily ever after in it. You are surrounded by your friends and family and things are just wonderful. Your fear may be in thinking that this may not happen and is saving for that dream home or apartment actually worth it?

So could your fear just be a story in your mind? You may not feel totally worthy of something so you begin to fear the outcome.

This brings us to reality and accepting that you live in the real world and that life happens for good or for bad. Yes, you cannot control your life but you can control certain events in it.

For example when you lose weight you are often told to imagine what you will look like once you lose 50 pounds. So you start envisioning how you will look, you begin to look forward to your transformation. This motivates you to reach your goal and get to the point where you have lost the weight.

You want to apply these same principles to your fears. Are you terrified of buying that house because of the cost? Or is it because you are not sure of how strong your relationship with your spouse is? You are imagining that a new home in a new neighborhood will fix all your problems. This is not likely to happen, but you are dreaming that owning a home solves unhappiness.

What you want to learn to do is to use your imagination to conquer your fears. If you are frightened of flying start imaging yourself buying a plane ticket, then arriving at the airport and then boarding the plane and finally taking off. ttet as detailed as you can so that you can feel your surroundings. At the same time
40

imagine yourself enjoying this experience. The more you do this the more your fear will dissipate.

Many people turn to hypnosis as a way to deal with fear. If your fears are irrational and affecting your life in a huge way then you may want to consider seeking professional help.

The word hypnosis may have a bad rap and immediately makes you think of someone dangling a watch in front of you. You may think that while hypnotized you lose control of what you say and do. This is so far from the truth.

A clinical hypnotherapist helps you discover the causes of your fear and then can help you eliminate it. This is done by conditioning your mind to respond differently to the stimulus.

Many people have used this type of hypnosis to cure their fears. Adele used it to help her overcome her stage fright and Tiger Woods is reported to see a hypnotherapist regularly.

If you feel as though your fear is firmly embedded in your mind then taking this path of action could be extremely beneficial to you. Think of seeing a hypnotherapist as a way to wrap up your fear, put it into a box and throw away the key forever.

Is Your Fear in Your Mind - Exercises

Do the following exercises in a quiet place, you may even wish to light candles or have soft music playing.

1. Think about a pleasant experience where you feel happy and relaxed.

2. Slowly start to visualize your fear.

3. Breathe deeply and take control of your fear.

4. Visualize yourself opening a strong box and placing your fear inside it.

5. Now close the box and tie it up with a rope or chain and lock it with a strong key.

6. Put the box away and see yourself walking away from it. Your fear is now locked out of your mind.

How to Prevent a Fear Relapse

Once you have conquered your fear you want to be aware of any signs that you might be headed for a possible lapse. A lapse is where you suddenly revert back to your old ways and let your fears control you. A lapse can happen because you are tired, anxious or stressed out about something.

A relapse though, is more significant and is something that you don't want to happen. Many people experience a relapse after going through a brief lapse. It is easy to see yourself as a failure, and this triggers old behavior patterns.

To prevent a full relapse you need to understand what your warning signs are. These can be different for each person but the most common signs include:

- Feeling stressed out
- Being given more work than you can cope with
- Not sleeping enough

- Experiencing a major life change either good or bad, a new baby or a death in the family

- Feeling anxious

You need to be aware of these changes in your feelings and be prepared to take action. Action steps that you can do include:

- Spending some quiet time alone

- Reading a book

- Taking a hot bath

- Enjoying a massage

- Meeting up with a friend and chatting

- Going for a drive in the country

Depending upon your fears you must be ready to acknowledge that situations may crop up at any time that may spur this fear in you. If you are frightened of dogs, you never know when you might run into one. You want to plan for this in advance as much as possible. This way when you are suddenly faced with this fear you are equipped with tools to handle it.

Your coping tools could be things such as not running away from the animal. Standing still and taking a deep breath. Tell the owner that you don't like dogs so they don't bring it any near.

If an old fear suddenly reappears, acknowledge that this has happened and record your feelings. While you may still feel scared, maybe your feelings weren't as intense? Did you fight the fear to flee? All of these things are positive reactions and show that you are managing your fear on a much better level than before.

With a fear such as one of dogs or of just meeting people in social situations, you know you will be faced with them again and again. By having a plan of action in place you can learn to minimize your fear and eventually quell those feelings in your stomach. Why not try to practice in advance for this to happen to you? Even if you just sit and imagine the situation you can then walk yourself through your responses in your mind. By doing this repeatedly your responses are more likely to become automatic when faced with them in real time.

Preventing a Relapse - Exercises

Write out the fear that you have just conquered in a positive way.

1. I have just conquered my fear of

_____

2. Next write down three situations that might occur where your fear could resurface. This could be going to the park

and running into a dog or going to a business function and meeting people.

a.

_____

b.

_____

c.

_____

3. Make a list of three or four coping tools that you can use.

a.

_____

b.

_____

c.

_____

d.

_____

CONCLUSION

This book and accompanying exercises can help you overcome your fears. You will be able to tell if you are dealing with a fear or if you are suffering from a panic attack. No matter which applies to you, you now have useful tools you can put in place and deal with these issues.

Remember no two people experience fear in the same way. What works for someone else may not necessarily work for you. It is important to understand that recognizing your fear is a major breakthrough in overcoming it. Once you can identify the what, you can work on the how and why. It is often helpful to discuss your fears with someone else. This might be your spouse, a close friend or even a counselor or therapist. Whatever you do, do not feel ashamed of your fear. Most people have had to deal with at least one fear in their life time, if not more. You are definitely not alone.

Make sure you take the time to complete each exercise and repeat them if necessary. Writing out your thoughts and feelings is extremely therapeutic – more so than talking about them.

Thank you again for taking the time to read this book and feel free to contact me if you have any further questions.

Printed by Libri Plureos GmbH in Hamburg, Germany